Nov 7

For

Thank you a...
for being a...
in poetry and
life!
with gratitude,
Jennifer
Murray

EVERY

INADEQUATE

NAME

To Jenn
Thanks so much

NICK THRAN

EVERY INADEQUATE NAME

POEMS

A 4 A.M. BOOK

INSOMNIAC PRESS

LIBRARY AND ARCHIVES CANADA CATALOGUING IN PUBLICATION

Thran, Nick, 1980-
Every inadequate name / Nick Thran.

Poems.
ISBN 1-897178-27-1

1.Title.

PS8639.H73E94 2006   C811'.6   C2006-903862-7

The publisher gratefully acknowledges the support of the Canada
Council, the Ontario Arts Council, and the Department if Canadian
Heritage through the Book Publishing Industry Development Program.

Printed and bound in Canada

Insomniac Press
192 Spadina Avenue, Suite 403
Toronto, Ontario, Canada, M5T 2C2
www.insomniacpress.com

Cover design: Mike O'Connor
Text design and typesetting: Alysia Shewchuk
Cover and author photo: Dave Fraser

   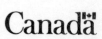

Carl Leggo
Jan./08
Promising!

This first one is dedicated to my sister, Robyn

CONTENTS

. . . No need,
he thought, to see the bell. It was not the bell
he was trying to find, but the angel lost
in our bodies. The music that thinking is.
He wanted to know what he heard, not to get closer.
— Jack Gilbert, "Haunted Importantly"

. . . Then you remember
the necessary and sufficient. This isn't it,
but you don't know where else to begin.
— Sue Sinclair, "Roses"

I

THE BLANK-LEAVED BOOK

I draft choral arrangements for tectonic plates.
I'd forgot to mention a few important
points: I was there at the gravesite
but did not bring my shovel,
I've never wept in a twentieth-century
building for anything other
than my own lost loves and friends.
Please, don't tell the architects.
Stones groan like a stomach ache
when they move. Bones tick
like a clock hand when
you tap them with a blade.

I think I'll split a pomegranate
and display the halves like dentists' x-rays
to a patient, star-filled night.
I think I'll diagnose the earth
with an affliction it has learned to cope with.
When I say, *I will never forgive you*
for letting it come to this,
you won't speak. You'll already know.

You and a friend are listening to music.
Pop Music. You know what Pop Music is –
though you may not like it.
Forget you. This is about falling in love
with something dated.
About leaving, losing touch, then years
later hearing that same love skewed
in a new band's blood. About turning
the volume up, and pressing repeat
until you're touched again.

This is about wave, new wave, and new
new wave. How your first time lasted exactly
two minutes and thirteen seconds –
the perfect length, you thought.
Awkwardness, elation, guilt, and confusion
key to a verse/chorus,
rising and falling. Anywhere
and anytime. Over again
and again and again and again.

I'm sick of this song, your friend says.
This must be the worst music
ever invented. When was the last time
the sugar wore off? The last time
you looked him straight in the eye
and told him how you heard this same song
sung by a boy
at the edge of a candlelit dock
over the lake where his best friend drowned?

You don't know shit, you want to say.
You don't know how Pop sounds.

For anyone who's held the door open for someone
with a particularly heavy load. Anyone

pretending to watch the weather report
while a stranger's delicates swirl
around in that first meeting between
her Friday of lovemaking,
and her Wednesday, say,
alone with an *In Style,* munching Corn Bran
straight from the box,
and trimming her fingernails.

I am trying to finish a Russian novel,
but this hum is a pacemaker
and this is for anyone who has buried
their hands into clean clothes and felt
the memory of two mugs
from last Saturday morning
still warming the palms of their hands.

Isn't the temperature balmy?
Don't all of our pockets call like bells?
Doesn't pouring powdered detergent sound
like the slanted roof that first day in spring
when all the old snow fell?

This is for all the proprietors
who close up late, know laundry is often done
when there is nothing left to do.

This is for the Coin O'Rama
after it empties. The last one there –
the Korean woman with slender fingers
picking lint and old dryer sheets deep
from the bowels –

how final the moment must feel

when she closes the lid
of the trash can
filled with clouds.

Say, *yellows, greys, dark blues,*
and dress yourself in them.

Say, *my bones are the fortress that will not fall,*
and scrub-shine those teeth with vigour.

Say, *dry, unkissable lips,*
and then balm them.

Say, *snow.* Say, *drizzle.* Say, *wind,*
and condition

according to memory, to the image outside.
Voila!

You are prepared for the weather.
Say, *there will be subtle, unforeseen shifts.*

Right shoe, say. *Left shoe,* say.
Double knots.

Remember to lock the doors when you leave.
Whisper, *I am always behind you.*

Like R, after throwing the metal pipe clear across
the surface of the ice pond, bragging he too
could slide it. His knees bloodied up
in the breakage. Like C in the psych ward, saying,
"Look, I'm holed up here, but you know, I'm not crazy" –
tongues and their infinite variables. They rolled us.
We couldn't bring ourselves to tell A, the exchange student,
that "Does a bear shit in the woods?" is not
a common expression. We liked that he trusted his phrase book;
the idea of scouring downtown haunts truly foreign,
nuzzling the language out. Like me thinking
I've a move or two down pat, till she says,
"No hon', there hon', yes hon', that's where
the song is." Bears in a balancing act
on the slick. Go there crazy, the foreign implores,
just finish your sentence, your riff.

In the green petri dish of Experiment Football
everything looks either cute or ridiculous; this
depends on whether or not you're a parent

with some stake in the game; or, like us,
are just suckers for chaos
and helmets like snowballs, or skulls

from a species of fat-headed humans
wanting no more from their children
than to *kick some ass, bust some heads,*

get out and do 'em proud. Here,
shoulder pads can't find any shoulders.
Equipment blurs the line

between protection and burden –
which a few of us up in the bleachers,
in our own way, understand.

In the green petri dish of Experiment Football
one little monster realizes he runs
faster than anyone, and when it happens

he's weightless, ruleless, and the distance he gains
is infinite yardage. He breaks the seam,
the tie, our hearts,

breaks those things once,
that's all it takes to tip us
from green out to grey streets,

our spirits scrambling
through these bodies we're given –

pushing the bones aside
and every inadequate name.

The poem won't ever save the world.
The poem won't even raise you up
from your sickbed and make you feel better.
But the poem is trying to do what it can.
It is learning the fiddle, knitting a homemade scarf,
riding a Bengal tiger through a field of ragweed
and doing somersaults off of a bridge.

The poem has even mastered some magic tricks:
one with a hand axe, a rat, and a cantaloupe, another
with a simple deck of cards.
It is satisfying two, no, make that three
beautiful women at once. They can hardly believe
the poem can keep on like this. You can hear them singing
like honey and rivers and wine.

The poem is putting fresh, crisp sheets on the bed.
It bought you a new pair of socks to wear
every day for the rest of your life.

The poem is making an honest man
out of a shyster. It is teaching your sister to read.
It is planning a vacation: one week in Bali
followed by three days gambling at Caesar's Palace
and buying tickets for the novel, the short story, the drama
and all of the poem's other friends.

The poem is walking on one bad leg
with an injured orangutan slung over its shoulder.
It is spending long nights alone in a room,
digging its fingernails into the wall, and talking to ghosts,
and reading Hegel, and beading a necklace
made entirely of scorpions who have solemnly sworn
never to hurt you. You're going to have to trust the poem
despite its shortcomings. Word is, it knows a couple of secrets
about life and beauty and eternity and grace
I couldn't possibly ever hope to reveal
speaking to you, as I am.

How to hold onto summers in Andalucía?
Thaisma, I am still a young man
with a mouth full of sand. I want the wisdom
of old age early. To distance myself
far enough from the past
to tell you: unborn, invisible daughter,
your father was playing at more
than games. He went
to the volleyball net and writhed
like a beached fish.
He kept the sun in the air
with the last bit of breath
from his gills.

THE BEAR CLAW TUB

Oh, and another thing, under no circumstances are you to ever
write about any of this in your poems. — Anonymous

Old-fashioned, dragging its bloat porcelain
across the linoleum floor. A mythological creature
left to decorum. Empty, it was where I imagined
a child playing pirates. Full, it was where I entered
to let off steam. The day's last hour slouched round.
Nothing born. The sort of place suicides happen
in movies, or where murder victims are found.
The tiny hairs on my neck would stand on end
when I came up from its warmth. Best on nights
I'd return home stinking, sweating, having
hurt who I loved most. I listened to the faucet drip,
those heavy paws on the linoleum floor. I was no good
at keeping my trap shut then. I'm still not. So long. *Roar.*

Driving through the outskirts of Calgary,
I am suddenly lost to the Eagles.

A wrong turn on Eagle Trace,
I end up on Eagle Rock
when I should be heading north on Eagle Ridge –
or south. It hardly matters now,
surrounded as I am by the low-toned
plumage and stucco –
nothing the cashier downtown
at the Stop & Go prepared me for
when I asked directions.

Eagles perched side by side, three-tiered.
On Eagle Lake, I saw one child
pummel a garage with a puck in a series
of well-timed slappers.
I wanted to shout from the car window, *Run!*
But where would he go
except into the mouths of the Eagles?

Now barrelling in to a snow-blind west
on Eagle Park, and no distinguishable feature
to lead me to my aunt's house for dinner,
where we'll talk about mortgage and credit,
how life's moving forward, or just spiralling down
into the gullet of an unkempt secret we figured

we'd arrive at one day;
what it was like in new classes, careers;
or stories from times before
the sprawl of suburbia,
before suvs, digital cable –
feathers unwittingly followed here

to Eagle Nest,
326 Eagle Nest –
before we were devoured.

Forgive these fat red flakes of snow
backlit by the motel's neon awning.

The little dog curled up in the cave
of a worn leather jacket,

and whatever else I may have
at one time or another
mistaken for the heart.

Forgive the moon, white cellular phone
on a black sheet – I'd been startled from

the recurring dream
where I am a cymbalist,

bare palmed, back row, and we're working
through a rendition of Beethoven's twenty-fifth Sonata.

Look Dog, I haven't forgotten the music.
Forgive me. I'm applauding the violins.

II

THE BACKWARDS BASIC

I'd like to feed the parking meter
a couple of more dimes.

I'd like to sit with you
down at the harbour,

I'd like to take my time,
I wanna take my time . . .

I should have propped something else beside it –
an empty can, or the last half of my sandwich.
As it stands, the cricket's size grows in the telling,
spreads like the news, years ago, of abandoned stacks
of dirty magazines stowed at the creek behind
the street where I grew up. When my bicycle tires
edged over the lip, boys were already clutching the rain-
soaked pages in their fists, the ink of my first
glimpses of flesh were already starting to pale,
to bleed into the leaves. Seriously, we'd say
in the schoolyard, it was the coolest. Later, actual

clothing would melt off actual flesh; yes, melt,
not just fall to the floor, because, seriously, she
was the hottest. Then gossip flares up in the yard's
kindled corners. When she finally calls up, crying,
I don't relay how her *how could yous* clutched
at my throat, pinned me to the receiver, silent, ashamed,
because I knew I'd been the worst.

Then what? I left, took a few bum jobs
humping rich peoples' luggage, spent two years
in Seoul, Korea, navigating through crowds
where, for the first time, I was the tallest,
so I stuck out to this gorgeous backpacker

who speaks fluent Italian, recites whole blocks
of the Inferno aloud, and moved in with her
as soon as I came home, because, seriously,
it felt like the real thing. Though I'm no longer sure

"real" is the right word, because it's years on,
and I'm no longer sure of this house, or this town,
or my job, and with her, lately, well let's just say
this stretch has been tough. So I stuff the last three
cans of a six-pack, a camera, and a sandwich
into a knapsack, set out to hike along a creek
where leaves brushing against my bare forearms
still feel erotic. Rambling, I turn this corner to find

there, on a bare patch of dirt, the world's biggest cricket,
this freakishly massive thing, and clutch at my mouth
as the air fills with the orchestral swell of its legs,
and gather myself enough to snap a single photo
before it leaps so high I think it must be heading
into someone else's life. *Shit*, I whisper further on,
realizing my shot on the bare patch will show nothing
of its largeness. Hear myself having to try to explain,
struggling, because it was amazing, and, seriously,
I've never been able to help myself. One way or another,
I will have to try to tell her every single thing.

For the lucky few who knew Gurdeep from the beginning, the question on all of our minds was: what would be done with the jarred sheep's brain he kept in the dorm?

Swiped from the display case during a group experiment in Biology, the brain was tucked away under the crest of his private-school blazer. It glowed for months in the dull light of the dormitory fridge. On breaks from texts and tennis sets he'd let us pass it around the same way we passed around pornography, or bottles of Silent Sam. We'd loosen our stiff white collars and try to preserve some sense of a world past those manicured hedges.

Nuge suggested a projectile launch at the Dean's face during our weekly assembly. Andrew offered the steamed vat of Monday's caf chili – nobody truly understanding the decision was Gurdeep's, who, after a time, chose simply to place his brain inside the bookcase of a girl he thought was beautiful, to gauge where he was in that world by placing what he'd concealed, minutes before History, into another consciousness.

FOUND: SALSA INSTRUCTIONS WITH FRANK RAMOS

She left her child alone in her crib, to dry up like soil in a summer drought, while she slaked her thirst for salsa dancing.
— Justice David Watt

A dancer too obviously "slaking a thirst"
is not dancing the salsa
correctly. This is standard tempo:
four quarter notes, one-hundred-sixty beats
per minute. The overeager often waver
between melody and rhythm.
They tend to forget we dance this largely
with our feet barely leaving the ground.

Too many turns in succession in a single direction
will make you dizzy. Hip movement stems
from proper legwork. The faster the beat,
and it's picking up now, the smaller our steps should be.

No forced movements, upper body rocking,
whiplash. Mirror my movements. We'll start
with the "backwards basic." Tense arms,
pressure between us. This pressure
feels good, looks good to observers. Makes it possible
to perform moves that would be
impossible otherwise – double crossed

holds, for example, our arms intertwined,
or some of the freestyle fancy
footwork known as "shines."

Grandpa swilled the hard stuff,
    trying to forget the black cough
of a coal mine, the pang
    of a bullet in his thigh.
But mine are lighter times,
    calling for lighter drinks
and Saturday nights at Amnesia.
    He'd have told me I've got it way too easy,
but I've been waiting in this lineup
    for what seems like forever –
a pocket full of someone else's money
    and the need to dance. Inside
we raise our glasses
    to make a toast
though nobody has anything to say.
    Then a woman puts her hand on my leg
and praise is due *to our good health,*
    and the condom machine by the toilet.

On the dance floor I wonder
        how Grandpa would've moved
packing all that weight.
        But the bass line's loud
and the strobe light's on
        and things have a way
of disappearing. At midnight
        the foam guns spray the floor
and we're all atheists, wet,
        on ecstasy, sliding
through each other's bodies
        – angels at Club Amnesia –
engaged in the art
        of forgetting the absence
of any real memory in us.

He walked down to the shore of La Linea and saw
what the Levante had done to the coast: an orange
split open over a stone, flies burrowing through
the flesh. He tiptoed around it in silence.

To the left, countless oranges bobbing
in the still, grey expanse of the Mediterranean,
To the right, the Great Rock
of Gibraltar. The narrow passage between it

and the top lip of Africa. Tangier.
Beyond that he pictured the Atlantic Ocean –
tumultuous waters – and sensed
it was time to go, and although

he knew where, made a promise
to love that place. Scatter fruit over the ground.

Bloor Street at sunset, easily
the most romantic street in the world.
Bloor is the colour of the sky, blue
but with the hard "r" of a fire
raging from the tail end of a day that drags
the work world back home to the boroughs.
I hope it is Friday, steak night, the family
gathered around Bloor flesh, sinews of strained
muscle, and wine like the blood they have spent
all week to meet and laugh and eat
and drink themselves back in.
I hope there is *Scrabble*, and a child, bleary-eyed
from an afternoon playing *Halo* (bodies
Bloored to bits, the level completed) hits "grateful"
on a triple-word-score, and Bloors his parents
with what they thought he never knew.
Once in a Bloor moon, the joke goes, and mother
rubs his hair. Then she and her husband head
to bed and make love. That's "B" for the bed,
"l" for the love, and the "o!" and the "o!"
a string upon which they wish
they could balance forever,
but they know it is temporal
like sunrise over the most romantic
street in the world. The conductor
saying, *Bloor Street, Bloor Street, Bloor.*

THOUGHTS WHILE DRIVING A STRETCH OF MOUNTAIN ROAD, LISTENING TO A TAPE OF PABLO NERUDA READING "LAS ALTURAS DE MACHU PICCHU"

¡El muro, el muro!

A grainy tape, as though he's gargling
worried stones in his throat.
As if he may never get any of this
across to us clearly again. Stones within stones,
that's one translation. Having lived
in Andalucía for awhile, my grip
on the tongue should be better.
My driving should also be better.
This is the same stretch of road
where I once killed a deer. Veered too close
to the ditch and had to crank the wheel
back around, at which point you could not distinguish
the driver's side mirror from its head.

The bloat dispenser of this blood.

That's Nathaniel Tarn's translation
in the Vintage Book of World Poetry.
Tarn within Neruda. Reading the text
is like separating bits of broken skull
from broken bits of glass.
It is like travelling the same stretch over again
with his scratched-up voice in the deck,
believing *that* would clear my head.

If you've ever collided with something like *that*
then you know about phantoms,
about memory cleaving – shrubs
become deer, criss-cross in the dark –
about the subjunctive-present tense
to what's no longer there.

Driving, I often imagine colliding
with Pablo, or at least some crude form
of him. I could have learned a lot more.
I worry I might be putting too much of myself
inside this. Say, just let this one be what it is:
a Lumina parked on the side of the road
and a dead deer. A driver weeping
into his steering wheel. Stone above stone above stone.

It has been a struggle. Mother meant trying
to learn Spanish, but also listening
to the dispute pulsing down
through the hardwood floor
of the flat above our heads.

Neither of us really knew what was up
until an open-palm blow
broke the language barrier, and Mother,
who tries hard to do good in this world,
marched upstairs,
banged on their door till it opened
enough for her to ask
in a friendly, foreign voice
for *azucar,*
the Spanish word for sugar
she'd made a point to learn before *bastard,*
prison, abuse,
and *asshole, you leave her alone.*

Though reluctant
the man did find a little.
But she said it took him more
than a bit of time
to search out the pantry,
as she stood in the foyer listening
to soft weeping from another room.

My mother knew the word *gracias*.
Used the azucar to bake
her world-famous banana bread: a recipe
dug up after each
of the moments she calls
in our native tongue, a crisis.

That night she cut the pieces thick.
After they'd cooled, placed two
on a bone white china plate, and whispered
through that beautiful silence:
they are okay now

to eat. Azucar
never tasted so sweet,
was never so easy to swallow.

Staring at your stylist's black eye
        in the mirror
while she struggles
        to make you appear
beautiful,
        you slowly become
comfortable with it.
        Elvis on the stereo croons,
Oh Moody Blue,
        tell me am I getting through?

He didn't. As to *her* significant others'
        whereabouts,
you figure he's probably hovering
        like thick cloud
over a cocktail umbrella
        inside some peeler
where even flesh can't light the room.

She tries to sell you blonde highlights.
     Tsks your current unkempt style,
and decides it would be easiest
     to just go on and do
what it is that we normally do.

Cold sheers trim the neckline clean.
     She promises you'll leave this place
a brand new you.
     The jar
of sanitizer glows.
     Electric. Unreal. Blue.

Inner Harbour. A busker takes to the skin.
A pigeon holds a corn chip up to the sun
and thrashing (just wildly enough), works
the entire thing down its throat.

You have a bag full of crow feathers
and chicken wire. You're making wings
for a six-year-old boy on the mainland.

In this light, the sea shimmers like foil.
The reflection off one quarter can be so strong
you'd swear the fedora overflowed with silver.

In this light, it feels good just to lie like that
for an entire afternoon.

III

EDGEWATER

Coastline Variation #76

Already at the end
of a rail-less walk on the breakwater:
Eyes closed, we slip through
a frayed net of sea-kelp.

Oil rigs cross-hatch
the places we've come from.
Deep breaths of water salt-scour our lungs.

Who retrieves the antique harmonica
from the bottom?
Who lost it there?

In this fathomable darkness,
I can believe
we are one person –

lips to the mouthpiece, the harmonica singing.

Upstairs, your great uncle is coughing.
You are the creek that runs underneath
this foundation, the creek
you drove to with him
through miles of dusty mill roads
one day in midsummer, for a taste
of the freshest water ever –
one more reason a man might stay out here
forever, or at least till he finds a good patch
of blueberry bushes, and there is this stone
off of the cutbank he wants to carve
his address into. He's glad you're here.
It will take two of you to lift it.

Picture your great aunt back at the house
building a day around sunflower stalks
and the snow globe collection,
which needs to be polished.
So what if his cough wasn't born
of a dream of the desert,
didn't bloom out from the industrial chuff
of the city. You came back that day
with four full jugs, blue blood on your hands,
and the stone that sat so heavy
in the back of his old pickup
it set the steering column right.

Cough born of knowing a man
has to struggle. Cough born of choosing to stay
in spite of that; learning back roads so well
there are no maps or second guesses.

Now that the creek is rising towards him,
understand why he must stop
the water from filling his lungs, his sleep.
Feel how desperately he still wants to wake up
tomorrow in Edgewater,
how good that glass from the bottom
of the fourth jug will taste. There is stone to be carved.
There will be time for the flood of tears when he's gone.
He will be carried away, and you'll miss him.

Windows open a crack, I recline
inside the Yukon. AC off,
we'll need all of the battery's burn time
for the long drive out of camp.

M., the land out here is soft,
and there's a few plots left to plant.
Off-days I sit stoned with a mix tape,
the choice cuts of Kid A and Amnesiac,

and slap at the myriad mosquitoes
that sneak in through the slits.
I pile the dead ones up on the dash. The ones
still struggling for breath, I leave to squirm

in the cup-holder. I'm exhausted,
been camped out here so long my dreams
are mechanical – three steps, spike, pull,
plant the root, stomp – even my downtime

is staked to the dirt. Great big holes
in the mess tent tarp mark where
black bears have made their daily run
at what passes here for food.

The land out here is soft, which means
I'll make bank; don't mind my conscious self
temporarily lost. Not much point dwelling
on the what-abouts anyway. It is *hot*,

and I'm bitten, and it's contract work,
so no matter how fast I'm going,
the crew chief still drives by screaming:
Christ, Nick, is that the best that you've got?

(Alone, baked on some powerful
B.C. pot, a bare patch on a brain scan,
with one specific function to perform on one specific plot.)
Well, to be perfectly honest, it's not.

Off-days are rife with mosquitoes.
During the week I can't let their presence
intrude on my planting, or even exist
as afterthoughts. They swarm like memories

of someone abandoned, or a friend
who disappeared figuring the forest
that grew up around us had to be chopped.
(I'm not here to moralize,

asshole, I'm not.) When the bears pace
the perimeter, I fire two quick shots.
That starts them running. Invariably,
the mess tent still ends up shredded.

You're here in my thoughts.
Contract's up in August.
I'm sick of this, M. Write back
when you're actually ready to talk.

Even the ecstasy is manufactured.
    We've doled out our twenties
on this coastline, pooling what little we know
    of constellations:
Orion's Belt. The Big Dipper. The small.
    Exhausted, we invent the Trimsaw
of Cranbrook, Karina's Slide Guitar.
    Think for a minute about what our fathers have made
of this sky. All that comes to mind
    is television: The A-Team, Mr T.
I make no apologies. We gather what scraps we can,
    rummaging over this junk-
yard of stars. The end
    of our labour: an armoured
El Dorado, our surefire plan to plow
    all the clear way through the darkness.

A woman named Yael la Rose.
A handyman named Jesus.

When she swam that morning,
the sun rose, a blowfish burst in the water.

He folds up a photo of five moored boats,
pockets the coast of La Linea.

The name is a wake that the flesh leaves behind.
The flesh is a visible shiver.

Never mind the seventy-five cent charge
per extra topping. Give me everything
the chef can stuff between the folds
and, somehow, still manage to close.
I'll wait. Listen to dazed suits mutter
their litanies into cups of no cream
and no sugar. To a mother, on the cell to her child,
trying to explain in the simplest terms
what cremation means. Steam
rises from the omelette station, shrouds
the chef – his job's mystique
cranking up with the heat – crumbled feta
in one hand, diced ripe tomato in the other,
and a furrow in his brow,
as the methodic whirl of a fan blade
reminds him of the woman back home
who will sponge grease from his arms
with the same precision, the same careful strokes,
whenever his shift at the station
of impossible omelettes is done.

It's when the body turns into air
and rises to heaven, she explains.
When the world fills up with so much other stuff,
spirits like grandpa's go to a different,
more beautiful place – where there's space
for everyone, but his memory is what we keep here
in our hearts, where there's always room.

My omelette arrives. Impossibly, everything
I have paid for is in it. Even a bit of fried
potato to one side. Hats off to the chef,
who by now has moved
seamlessly on to the dishes.

A sigh at the end
of each word that she whispers:

La playa. Las estrellas. Mira. Mira.

A sigh at the end
as she draws you in closer:

Ahora.

There is a man who will dive.

Then there's the flat-out refusal
to even listen to any music recorded
after nineteen-sixty-eight.
The stance our modern Pop's been all fluff
since then, a permanent fall/melt cycle.
That these retread troubadours won't ever fill
the mainstays' giant holes.

Poor schmucks. It's hard to feel for them
today, walking from your house north
on Clinton – a light snowfall, and Jens
Lekman on my headphones giving the air
a touch of the glockenspiel in it.

This not the first snow, but this the first snow
I had kissed you. A jingle-jangle, sure,
but met with a wide-eyed, open look –
my, *was that really a tambourine!?*

your indelible tracks through the blank-leaved book.

BIRD TIME

I've nothing to say to the moon.
Still, I want to talk.
— William Matthews

I

The streetlamp's light on the cherry tree dresses
the night in a pink feather boa.

It all looks ridiculous from where I'm standing.
That's part of the reason I called.

II

I feel like those punks in their Acuras
out stealing signs: the signs

that tell us where the playgrounds end
and the loading

and unloading zones begin. Don't say
the wall in the shed where they're nailed doesn't read

like a call to prayer,
like the poem that repeats its directions

again, and again to the dark.

III

It's almost Bird Time. The name you gave
to when even the trucks racing on Burden Street

quiet their engines;
to when the glow-stick's impossible green

flickers out, and the hard-house,
the break-beats, the trance

grind their teeth into silence.

IV

Every frivolity the night wears
is being removed.

I need you.

At this hour my hands
are at least as good as wings.

"How Pop Sounds" was written as a homage of sorts to the title poem from Philip Levine's collection *What Work Is* (Alfred A. Knopf, 1992)

"How Pop Sounds pt 2 (The White Album)" *The Dictionary of Word Origins* (Kyle Cathy Limited, UK, 1995) describes an album as "any blank-leaved book ..." The Jens Lekman CD I have in mind is *Oh You're So Silent Jens* (Secretly Canadian, 2005) recommended to me by my Australian friend Sonja Dechian.

The epigraph from "Thoughts While Driving a Stretch of Mountain Road..." translates simply as "The wall, the wall!" and is taken from Pablo Neruda's poem "The Heights of Machu Picchu."

A number of these poems were written with specific people in mind. In each of these cases they know who they are, with the exception of "Edgewater," which was written for Frank Schnider prior to his death. I miss you, Frank.

ACKNOWLEDGEMENTS

Many of these poems, often in earlier versions, first appeared in the following publications:

Event, Existere, The Fiddlehead, Forget, Grain, The Malahat Review, Versal (The Netherlands), *Coastline Variations* (Mosquito Press, 2004), and *Desire, Doom & Vice: A Canadian Collection* (Wingate Press, 2005)

Thank you to the editors of these publications, in particular to Matt Rader at Mosquito Press and Kent Bruyneel at both *Grain* and *Forget*, for early and ongoing enthusiasm.

The generosity of the Ontario Arts Council and the Banff Centre for the Arts gave me the time and energy to complete this manuscript, for which I am grateful.

To my friend and editor, Paul Vermeersch, I thank you for your faith and gentleness. Thanks also to Don McKay, Stan Dragland, and Sue Sinclair for bringing their attention and first-rate talents to the editorial process, and to Dave Fraser for the cover image.

Patrick Lane lit a fire. Mark Samcoe fanned the early flames. Elizabeth Bachinsky, Mercedes Batiz-Benet, Chris Wilson-Smith, and Darren Bifford have been constants, and their friendship and support continues to mean a great deal. I've hidden a longer list, I hope, in the poems.

My parents, Dennis and Anita Thran, my sister, Robyn Thran, and my brother, Craig Battle, are acknowledged breathlessly. I simply could not do this without their love and support.

Finally, *Dear Sue, I am really glad you are working here.*